BUDDHIST MONK WISDOM

Compiled by Barry Phillips

Knowledge is King

Published by
Knowledge Is King
Mortimer House
49 Church Street
Theale
RG7 5BX
United Kingdom

Telephone 01491 201530
Email sales@knowledgeisking.co.uk
www.knowledgeisking.co.uk

Buddhist Monk Wisdom
ISBN 978-1-7397139-1-1

Buddhist Monk Wisdom

4

Introduction

LONG BEFORE THE BIRTH of formal religions, storytelling was the vehicle for sharing age-old wisdom. Profound truths about life found their expression within these stories, legends and history. Stories introduced their listeners to a wonderful world of magic and mystery.

Stories have also long been the traditional medium of teaching and learning. Great masters such as Jesus and Buddha excelled in story-telling, and elders of every religion have shared their wisdom in stories around campfires and in places of worship.

Buddhism and Zen Buddhism are famous for using short stories to help Buddhist students develop a deeper understanding of reality. I think of Buddhism as a philosophy, or a school of thought. You can be Christian or Jewish, for example, and still find the Buddha's teachings both helpful and inspirational.

The stories will remind you how timeless and universal the search is to find truth, peace and freedom, to live with love and courage, and to be free from conflict and pain.

The Golden Buddha Within

IN BANGKOK THERE IS A GOLDEN statue of the Buddha that stands 9'8" tall and weighs 5.5 tons. The gold in the statue is worth approximately £250 million.

The statue was thought to have been built in 1403 and was revered by Buddhists for many hundreds of years. In 1757, the Burmese Army invaded Thailand. Facing complete annihilation, the Buddhist monks at the monastery hastily began covering their Golden Buddha with plaster and clay, which was painted and inlaid with bits of coloured glass, to make it look of little or no value to the invading army. During the invasion, all the monks were tragically murdered, but the Golden Buddha was left undiscovered.

The statue then survived centuries of storms, changes of government and political turmoil. Although the statue wasn't particularly beautiful, it was deeply revered. In its presence, people felt a soothing sense of comfort, of familiarity.

In 1957, the time came for the Monastery to receive some renovations. In preparation, the monks were preparing to move the statue. It was dry season and the air was particularly hot and arid. As the process began, one of the monks noticed a large crack on the surface of the statue. Curious, he beamed a light inside. Upon peering in, he discovered a golden light emanating from the crack. Immediately, he shared his discovery with his fellow monks. Shortly afterwards, a group of them gathered with hammers and chisels to chip away at the plaster and clay. Soon, the group's efforts revealed a great, great treasure, the largest golden statue of the Buddha known to exist today.

What I love about this story is that the statue was purposely covered over with plaster and clay so it could survive difficult times. Much in the same way, we cover our own innate well-being with defence strategies and coping mechanisms in order to survive our difficult times.

We are all like the golden Buddha. When we are born, we are pure, intuitive, and we shine with light. As we grow, we throw on layers of stories from other people's ideas and opinions; we buy into the belief that we are broken. We doubt our intuitive insights, and we start to cover up the golden light that is within us. We constantly buy products to make us feel better and worthier. We speak quietly and don't voice our opinions and beliefs so as not to disappoint those around us. We buy the clothes and cars we believe we should want, and we pursue the friendships we think we need to make us feel valid. We are so laden with clay we have forgotten our golden Buddha within.

As we peel away this covering, we reveal that all the treasures we seek are not outside but are within ourselves. We already have everything we need.

No Cows To Lose

ONE DAY THE BUDDHA WAS sitting with some of his monks in the woods. A distraught farmer approached.

"Monks, have you seen my cows?"

"No we have not," the Buddha responded.

The farmer continued, "I am distraught. I have only six cows and I don't know why, but this morning they all ran away. I have lost everything; how will I survive?"

The Buddha looked at him with compassion.

"Dear friend, we have been sitting here almost an hour and we have not seen any cows passing by. Maybe you should go and look in the other direction."

When the farmer was gone, the Buddha looked at his friends and smiled knowingly.

"Dear friends, you are very lucky," he said, "You don't have any cows to lose."

Stuff

A YOUNG MONK BOARDED AN overnight train heading to his new monastery in Europe.

The station master told him, "There has been a lot of theft recently. We take no responsibility for any loss."

This worried the young monk, because he had a lot of stuff. So, he lay awake, fearing the worst, staring at all his worldly possessions.

Finally, at 3:00am, he fell asleep. Waking with a start twenty minutes later, he saw that all his stuff was gone. He took a deep breath.

"Thank Buddha," he said. "Now I can sleep."

The Monk And The Samurai

ONE DAY A CONFLICTED SAMURAI was meandering down a dirt road. He was unkempt, dishevelled and nursing a hangover. Just as he was at rock-bottom, he noticed a monk approaching. The closer the monk got, the clearer it became that the monk knew holy secrets. When the monk passed him, the Samurai spoke up.

"Holy monk, I seek your guidance. I am depressed as I do not know what awaits me after this life. Please, can you tell me the difference between Heaven and Hell?"

The monk returned a look of disgust. "You are but a lonely, shameful Samurai. You kill with no mercy, your sword is rusty and you have nothing to offer the world. Why should I share such holy secrets with such a despicable man?"

Outraged, the Samurai unsheathed his sword. He had never experienced such anger, and he decided to strike down this secret-hoarding monk. He raised his sword and brought it down over the monk's head.

Just before contact, without flinching, the monk smiled.

"This is Hell", he said. You have given into anger and you are now possessed by it."

Realizing the lesson he just learned, a sense of remorse and humility came over the Samurai. He was ashamed by his actions. He immediately cast aside his sword and fell to his knees.

"Holy monk, please forgive me for my actions. I am unworthy of your presence. I will never raise my sword in anger again."

Smiling, the monk replied, "This, my dear Samurai, is Heaven. You are humble, and soon serenity will envelope you. Heaven and hell may await us after this life; however they are experienced throughout it. Some spend their entire lives wandering through Hell, waiting for Heaven, never realizing it's already within their grasp."

The Wise Master

THERE ONCE WAS MASTER who lived with a great number of student monks in a run-down temple. The students supported themselves by begging for food in the bustling streets of a nearby town. Some of the students grumbled about their humble living conditions.

In response, the old master said one day, "We must repair the walls of this temple, but since we occupy ourselves with study and meditation, there is no time to earn the money we will need. I have thought of a simple solution."

All the students eagerly gathered closer to hear the words of their teacher.

"Each of you must go into the town and steal goods that can be sold on for money," said the master. "In this way, we will be able to repair our temple."

The students were startled at this suggestion from their wise master. But since they respected him greatly, they assumed he must have good judgement and did not protest.

The wise master said sternly, "In order not to defile our excellent reputation by committing illegal and immoral acts, please be certain to steal when no one is looking. I do not want anyone to get caught."

When the teacher walked away, the students discussed the plan among themselves.

"It is wrong to steal," said one. "Why has our wise master asked us to do this?"

Another retorted, "It will allow us to repair our temple, which is a good thing."

They all agreed that their teacher was wise and must have a sensible reason for making such an unusual request.

So they set out eagerly for the town, promising each other that they would not disgrace their temple by getting caught.

"Be careful," they called to one another. "Do not let anyone see you stealing!"

All the students except one young monk set off for town. The wise master approached him and asked, "Why do you stay behind?"

The monk responded, "I cannot follow your instructions to steal where no one will see me. Wherever I go, I am always there watching. My own eyes will see me steal."

The wise master tearfully embraced the young monk.

"I was just testing the integrity of my students," he said. "You are the only one who has passed the test! Now quickly round up all the other monks before they reach the town!"

The young monk went on to become a wise master himself.

What Happens When We Die?

A NOVICE MONK WAS TALKING with a Zen master one day.

He asked the master, "What happens when we die?"

"I don't know," responded the Zen master.

This upset the young novice.

"But I thought you were a Zen master?"

The master replied, "I am a Zen master, but not a dead one!"

The Other Side

ONE DAY A YOUNG BUDDHIST on his journey home came to the banks of a wide river. Staring hopelessly at the great obstacle in front of him, he pondered for hours on just how to cross such a wide barrier.

Just as he was about to give up his pursuit to continue his journey he saw a great teacher on the other side of the river.

The young Buddhist yelled to the teacher, "Oh wise one, can you tell me how to get to the other side of this river?"

The teacher pondered for a moment, looked up and down the river and yelled back, "My son, you are on the other side!"

Your Teacup Is Full

ONCE, A LONG TIME AGO, there was a wise Zen master. People from far and near would seek his counsel and ask for his wisdom. Many would come and ask him to teach them, enlighten them in the way of Zen. He seldom turned any away.

One day an important man, a man used to command and obedience, came to visit the master.

"I have come today to ask you to teach me about Zen. Open my mind to enlightenment."

The tone of the important man's voice was one of someone used to getting his own way.

The Zen master smiled and said that they should discuss the matter over a cup of tea. When the tea was served the master poured his visitor a cup. He poured and he poured and the tea rose to the rim and began to spill over the table and finally onto the robes of the wealthy man.

Finally the visitor shouted, "Enough. You are spilling the tea all over. Can't you see the cup is full?"

The master stopped pouring and smiled at his guest.

"You are like this tea cup, so full that nothing more can be added. Come back to me when the cup is empty. Come back to me with an empty mind."

Peace Of Mind

ONE DAY BUDDHA WAS WALKING from one town to another town with a few of his followers. While they were travelling, they happened to pass a lake.

They stopped there and Buddha told one of his disciples, "I am thirsty. Do get me some water from that lake there please."

The disciple walked up to the lake. When he reached it, he noticed that some people were washing dirty clothes in the water and, right at that moment, a bullock cart started crossing through the lake. As a result, the water became very muddy and cloudy.

The disciple thought, "How can I give this muddy water to Buddha to drink?"

So he came back and told Buddha, "The water in there is very muddy. I don't think it is fit to drink."

After about half an hour, again Buddha asked the same disciple to go back to the lake and get him some water to drink. The disciple obediently went back to the lake. This time he found that the lake had absolutely clear water in it. The mud had settled down and the water above it looked fit to be consumed. So he collected some water in a pot and brought it to Buddha.

Buddha looked at the water, and then he looked up at the disciple and said, "See what you did to make the water clean. You let it be ... and the mud settled down on its own, and you got clear water... Your mind is also like that. When it is disturbed, just let it be. Give it a little time. It will settle down on its own. When it's calm, everything becomes clear. You don't have to put in any effort to calm it down. It will happen, and it is effortless."

The Monk And The Scorpion

TWO MONKS WERE WASHING their bowls in the river when they noticed a scorpion that was drowning. One monk immediately scooped it up and set it upon the bank. In the process he was stung. He went back to washing his bowl and again the scorpion fell in. The monk saved the scorpion and was again stung.

The other monk asked him, "Friend, why do you continue to save the scorpion when you know its nature is to sting?"

"Because," the monk replied, "to save it is my nature."

Right And Wrong

WHEN BANKEI, A ZEN MASTER, held his seclusion-weeks of meditation, pupils from many parts of Japan came to attend. During one of these gatherings a pupil was caught stealing.

The matter was reported to Bankei with the request that the culprit be expelled. Bankei ignored the case.

Later the pupil was caught in a similar act, and again Bankei disregarded the matter. This angered the other pupils, who drew up a petition asking for the dismissal of the thief, stating that otherwise they would all leave.

When Bankei had read the petition, he called everyone before him.

"You are wise brothers," he told them. "You know what is right and what is wrong. You may go somewhere else to study if you wish, but this poor brother does not even know right from wrong. Who will teach him if I do not? I am going to keep him here even if all the rest of you leave."

A torrent of tears cleansed the face of the brother who had stolen. All desire to steal had vanished.

The Zen Master And The Thief

RYOKAN, A ZEN MASTER, lived the simplest kind of life in a little hut at the foot of a mountain. One evening a thief visited the hut only to discover there was nothing in it to steal.

Ryokan returned and caught him.

"You may have come a long way to visit me," he told the prowler, "and you should not return empty-handed. Please take my clothes as a gift."

The thief was bewildered. He took the clothes and slunk away.

Ryokan sat naked, watching the moon.

"Poor fellow," he mused, "I wish I could give him this beautiful moon."

Two Monks
And A Woman

TWO MONKS WERE TRAVELLING together, a senior and a junior. They came to a river with a strong current where a young woman was waiting, unable to cross alone. She asks the monks if they would help her cross the river. Without a word and in spite of the sacred vow he'd taken not to touch women, the older monk picked her up, crossed, and set her down on the other side.

The younger monk joined them across the river and was aghast that the older monk had broken his vow but didn't say anything. An hour passed as they travelled on. Then two hours, then three. Finally, the now quite agitated younger monk could stand it no longer.

"Why did you carry the woman when we took a vow as monks not to touch women?"

The older monk replied, "I set her down hours ago by the side of the river. Why are you still carrying her?"

Buddha's Bowl

ONE TIME, BUDDHA WAS WALKING with a disciple, and everybody in town was criticising him, saying, "You're no good. You don't do this, you don't do that…"

The disciple said, "Buddha, doesn't it bother you that all these people are criticising you?"

Buddha waited until they got back to his home, then he took his bowl and moved it towards the disciple.

He said, "Whose bowl is it?"

The disciple said, "It's your bowl."

So Buddha moved it a little closer to the disciple.

"Whose bowl is it?"

"It's still your bowl," replied the disciple.

Buddha kept doing this, and the disciple kept saying, "It's your bowl, it's your bowl."

Then Buddha took the bowl and put it in the disciple's lap, and said, "Now whose bowl is it?"

The disciple said, "It's still your bowl."

"Exactly!" said Buddha. "If you don't accept this bowl, it's not yours. If I don't accept criticism, it's not mine."

Chop Wood, Carry Water

A YOUNG BOY BECAME A MONK. He dreamed of enlightenment and of learning great things. When he got to the monastery he was told that each morning he had to chop wood for the monks' fires and then carry water up to the monastery kitchen. He attended prayers and meditation, but the teaching he was given was rather sparse.

One day he was told to take some tea to the master in his room. He did so and the master saw he looked sad and asked him why.

The boy replied, "Every day all I do is chop wood and carry water. I want to learn. I want to understand things. I want to be great one day, like you."

The master gestured to the scrolls on shelves lining the walls.

He said, "When I started I was like you. Every day I would chop wood and carry water. Like you I understood that someone had to do these things, but like you I wanted to move forward. Eventually I did. I read all of the scrolls; I met with Kings and gave council. I became the master. Now,

I understand that the key to everything is that everything is 'chopping wood and carrying water' and that if one does everything mindfully, then it is all the same."

Enlightened

ONE DAY THE MASTER ANNOUNCED that a young monk had reached an advanced state of enlightenment. The news caused some stir. Some of the other monks went to see the young monk.

"We heard you are enlightened. Is that true?" they asked.

"It is," he replied.

"And how do you feel?"

"As miserable as ever," said the monk.

The master later explained, "Many people believe that with enlightenment come peace, power and a sense of knowing, but with each stage of enlightenment, we must still chop wood and carry water."

Awakening

A MODERN MASTER DESCRIBED how the Buddha had encouraged his monks by stating that those who practised diligently would surely be enlightened in seven days or, if not in seven days, then in seven months or seven years. A young American monk heard this and asked if it was still true. The master promised that if the young monk was continuously mindful without break for only seven days, he would be enlightened.

Excitedly, the young monk started his seven days, only to be lost in forgetfulness ten minutes later. Coming back to himself, he again started his seven days, only to once more become lost in mindless thought about what he would do after his enlightenment. Again and again he began his seven days, and again and again he lost his continuity of mindfulness.

A week later, he was not enlightened but had become very much aware of his habitual fantasies and wandering of mind - a most instructive way to begin his practise on the path to true awakening.

Slowing Down

ONE OF THE MONKS IN THE temple was well known for his zealousness and effort. Day and night he would sit in meditation, not stopping to even eat or sleep. As time passed he grew thinner and more exhausted. The master of the temple advised him to slow down, to take more care of himself. But the monk refused to heed his advice.

"Why are you rushing so? What is your hurry?" asked the master.

"I am after enlightenment," replied the monk, "There is no time to waste."

"And how do you know," asked the master, "that enlightenment is running on before you, so that you have to rush after it? Perhaps it is behind you, and all you need to encounter it is to stand still, but you are running away from it?"

Enlightenment

ZEN TEACHERS OFTEN TELL THE story of a young monk who asked a Zen master, "How long will it take me to attain enlightenment?"

The master thought for a few moments and replied, "About ten years."

The young monk was upset and said, "But you are assuming I am like the other monks and I am not. I will practice with great determination."

"In that case," replied the master, "twenty years."

Temper

A ZEN STUDENT CAME TO THE master and complained, "Master, I have an uncontrollable temper. How can I cure it?"

"You have something very strange," replied the master. "Let me see what you have."

"Just now I cannot show it to you."

"When can you show it to me?" asked the master.

"It arises unexpectedly," replied the student.

"Then," concluded the master, "it must not be your own true nature. If it were, you could show it to me at any time. When you were born you did not have it, and your parents did not give it to you. Think that over."

Do You Ever Get Angry?

THERE IS A STORY FROM THE Forest Monk tradition in Thailand about an extremely wise master who was both very intelligent and also had a deep experience of meditation.

The Thai King and Queen were his disciples at the time, so they regularly travelled to see the master to give him gifts and ask questions.

On one occasion, the King respectfully asked, "Master, do you ever get angry?"

It was a sensitive subject, because in Eastern religions calmness and composure is held to be very important. It is considered admirable not to let oneself get swept up in strong emotions and reactions.

The master replied in Thai.

"Mee, date mai aow."

This means something like, 'Anger arises, but nothing does it occupy.' It's not that we stop having those feelings we view as negative or difficult but that we stop identifying with them; we don't let them occupy us. Then they can no longer harm us, or make us do things we regret.

Being Human

HOGEN, A CHINESE ZEN TEACHER, lived alone in a small temple in the country. One day four travelling monks appeared and asked if they might make a fire in his yard to get warm.

While they were building the fire, Hogen heard them arguing about subjectivity and objectivity.

He joined them and said, "There is a big stone. Do you consider it to be inside or outside your mind?"

One of the monks replied, "From the Buddhist viewpoint, everything is an objectification of mind, so I would say that the stone is inside my mind."

"Your head must feel very heavy," observed Hogen, "if you are carrying around a stone like that in your mind."

The Journey's End

IKKYU, A ZEN MASTER, WAS VERY clever, even as a boy. His teacher had a precious teacup, a rare antique. Ikkyu accidentally broke this cup and was greatly perplexed. Hearing the footsteps of his teacher, he held the pieces of the cup behind him.

When the master appeared, Ikkyu asked, "Why do people have to die?"

"This is natural," explained the older man. "Everything has to die and has just so long to live."

Producing the shattered cup, Ikkyu said, "It was time for your cup to die."

Full Awareness

ZEN STUDENTS ARE WITH THEIR masters at least ten years before they presume to teach others. After ten years of apprenticeship, Tenno achieved the rank of Zen teacher. One rainy day, he went to visit the famous master Nan-in.

When he walked in, the master greeted him with a question, "Did you leave your wooden clogs and umbrella on the porch?"

"Yes," Tenno replied.

"Tell me," the master continued, "did you place your umbrella to the left of your shoes, or to the right?"

Tenno, confused, did not know the answer, and realized that he had not yet attained full awareness. So he became Nan-in's pupil and studied under him for six more years to accomplish this every-minute Zen.

Comparison

A MAN WHO HEARD ABOUT Buddha's life started longing to reach higher states within himself just like the Buddha had done. He met many masters and enquired about the Buddha, but he was not satisfied with their explanations. Then one person told him that there was a master living on the peak of a certain mountain who knew everything about the Buddha.

"Go ask him," the person told him.

So the man trekked up the difficult mountain path, finally reached the master's hut and entered. He noticed there were many disciples there already. The master was talking to his many disciples.

When he saw this man, the master asked him to come closer and asked him, "What do you want?"

The man said, "I am wandering in search of the Buddha's teachings. I have met many scholars, but nobody could fully answer my questions. I heard that you will be able to explain this better than all the others so I came to you."

"Oh! Please be seated. I will tell you after all of them leave," said the Zen master.

The man was satisfied. He concluded that this master must be really good for so many disciples to gather around him. The master spoke with each of his disciples and then sent them on their way. Finally, he came to the man and said,

"Come with me!"

He led the man across the slopes. After covering a certain distance, they came upon some vegetation before them.

The master pointed to it and said, "See that bamboo over there? See how short it is?"

The Monk replied, "Yes."

The master then pointed to other bamboo shoots that were off to the side and asked, "When you look at these, what do you see?"

The man said, "That bamboo is tall. This bamboo has not yet grown up and is short."

The master said, "These are bamboos!" and walked back to his hut.

Successorship

THE ZEN MASTER MU-NAN HAD only one successor. His name was Shoju. After Shoju had completed his study of Zen, Mu-nan called him into his room.

"I am getting old," he said, "and as far as I know, Shoju, you are the only one who will carry on this teaching. Here is a book. It has been passed down from master to master for seven generations. I also have added many points according to my understanding. The book is very valuable, and I am giving it to you to represent your successorship."

"If the book is such an important thing, you had better keep it," Shoju replied. "I received your Zen without writing and am satisfied with it as it is."

"I know that," said Mu-nan. "Even so, this work has been carried from master to master for seven generations, so you may keep it as a symbol of having received the teaching."

Shoju burnt it immediately.

Love Openly

TWENTY MONKS AND ONE NUN named Eshun, were practicing meditation with a certain Zen master.

Eshun was very pretty even though her head was shaved and her dress plain. Several monks secretly fell in love with her. One of them wrote her a love letter, insisting upon a private meeting.

Eshun did not reply. The following day the master gave a lecture to the group, and when it was over, Eshun arose.

Addressing the one who had written to her, she said, "If you really love me so much, come and embrace me now."

Too Much

AN AGED BUDDHIST MONK, who had lived a long and active life, was assigned a role at an academy for girls looking to become a "bhikkhuni", a fully ordained female monastic in Buddhism. In discussion groups he often found that the subject of love became a central topic.

This comprised his warning to the young women.

"Understand the danger of anything-too-much in your lives. Too much anger in combat can lead to recklessness and death. Too much ardour in religious beliefs can lead to close-mindedness and persecution. Too much passion in love creates dream images of the beloved - images that ultimately prove false and generate anger. To love too much is to lick honey from the point of a knife."

"But as a celibate monk," asked one young woman, "how can you know of love between a man and a woman?"

"Sometime, dear children," replied the old teacher, "I will tell you why I became a Buddhist monk."

Let Go

A WESTERN MONK AT A BUDDHIST monastery became frustrated by the difficulties of practise and the detailed and seemingly arbitrary rules of conduct the monks had to follow. He began to criticise other monks for sloppy practise and to doubt the wisdom of the teachings. At one point, he went to the master and complained, noting that even the master himself was inconsistent and seemed often to contradict himself in an unenlightened way.

The master just laughed and pointed out how much the monk was suffering by trying to judge others around him. Then he explained that his way of teaching is very simple.

"It's as though I see people walking down a road I know well. To them the way may be unclear. I look up and see someone about to fall in a ditch on the right-hand side of the road, so I call out to him, 'Go left, go left!' Similarly, if I see another person about to fall into a ditch on the left, I call out, 'Go right, go right!' That is the extent of my teaching. Whatever extreme you get caught in, whatever you get attached to, I say, 'Let go of that, too.' Let go on the left, let go on the right. Come back to the centre, and you will arrive at the true way."

True Surrender

ONE OF MY FAVOURITE TEACHINGS about the pathway of true surrender comes from a story about Ananda, the Buddha's attendant and deeply devoted disciple.

After the Buddha's death, when the great council of his enlightened followers was planned, Ananda was not invited. Although he had worked at it strenuously for years, he himself was not yet enlightened. And so on the eve of the council meeting, Ananda sat down to meditate, determined to practice vigorously all night, not stopping until he had attained full enlightenment.

But after many hours, he was only exhausted and discouraged. In spite of all his effort, there had not been even the slightest progress. So toward dawn, Ananda decided to surrender and to let go of striving and simply lie down and rest for a while. As the story goes, the moment his head touched the pillow, he was enlightened.

The Buddha
And The Acrobats

ONE DAY, WHEN THE BUDDHA was alive on earth, a very accomplished acrobat team came to see him. The team consisted solely of a grandfather and his granddaughter. They were famous all over the country, and performed daring acrobatic feats to large crowds. The two of them had been debating one crucial point for years, and finally decided to go to the Buddha, and ask him for help.

It was the grandfather who put their question to the Buddha.

"The feats we perform together are dangerous, and our safety is crucial," he told the Buddha.

"However, my granddaughter and I have different ideas about how to maximize our safety. My feeling is that each one of us should have our first attention on the other one. No matter what happens when we are working together, I have committed to taking care of my granddaughter first, even beyond concerns or fears for my own safety. This really seems to me to be the way that love works, and the best way to care for our safety.

My granddaughter disagrees. Her point of view is that we need to take care of ourselves first, no matter what is happening. Our first attention should be on our own safety.

We cannot reconcile our two points of view, so we have come to you, to ask for the blessings of your wisdom and clarity."

The Buddha smiled at both of them.

He turned to the grandfather and said, "How lucky you are to have a granddaughter with such intelligence. I invite you to really listen to her, for she is clear about this. You have been conditioned to another way of thinking which will not serve you here. Listen to the voice of this young one. Question your ingrained ideas about what love is.

How can you possibly help her if you yourself are in danger? Where will you stand? What kind of help can you offer her, if your foundation is shaking and trembling?

We would all do well to follow the wisdom of your granddaughter. Taking care of ourselves first is not selfishness, it is basic sanity."

The Mustard Seed

DURING BUDDHA'S TIME, there lived a woman named Kisa Gotami. She married young and gave birth to a son. One day, the baby fell sick and died soon after. Kisa Gotami loved her son greatly and refused to believe that he was dead. She carried the body of her son around her village, asking if there was anyone who can bring him back to life.

The villagers all saw that the son was already dead and there was nothing that could be done. They advised her to accept his death and make arrangements for the funeral. In great grief, she fell upon her knees and clutched her son's body close to her body. She kept uttering for her son to wake up.

A village elder took pity on her and suggested she consult the Buddha.

"Kisa Gotami, we cannot help you. But you should go to the Buddha. Maybe he can bring your son back to life!"

She immediately went to the Buddha's residence and pleaded for him to bring her son back to life.

"Kisa Gotami, I have a way to bring your son back to life."

"My Lord, I will do anything to bring my son back."

"If that is the case, then I need you to find me something. Bring me a mustard seed but it must be taken from a house where no one residing in the house has ever lost a family member. Bring this seed back to me and your son will come back to life."

Kisa Gotami went from house to house, trying to find the mustard seed.

At the first house, a young woman offered to give her some mustard seeds. But when Kisa Gotami asked if she had ever lost a family member to death, the young women said her grandmother died a few months ago.

She moved on to the second house. A husband had died a few years ago. The third house lost an uncle and the fourth, an aunt. She kept moving from house to house but the answer was always the same – every house had lost a family member to death.

Kisa Gotami finally came to realise that there is no one in the world who had never lost a family member to death. She now understood that death is inevitable and a natural part of life.

Forgiveness

THE CAMBODIAN BUDDHIST MONK Maha Ghosananda led the restoration of Buddhism in his homeland following the killing by the Khmer Rouge between 1976 and 1979 of all but 3,000 of the country's 60,000 Buddhist monks. Despite losing his entire family, including 16 siblings, he was at the forefront of efforts to reconcile Cambodia's opposing factions and encouraged forgiveness by their victims.

Maha opened a Buddhist temple in a barren refugee camp of the Khmer Rouge communists. There were fifty thousand villagers who had become communists at gunpoint and had now fled the destruction to camps on the Thai border. In this camp the underground Khmer Rouge camp leaders threatened to kill any who would go to the temple. Yet on its opening day more than twenty thousand people crowded into the dusty square for the ceremony. These were the sad remnants of families, an uncle with two nieces, a mother with only one of three children. The schools had been burned to the ground, the villages destroyed, and in nearly every family, members had been killed or taken away.

Maha began the service with the traditional chants that had permeated village life for a thousand years. Though these words had been silenced for eight years of war and the temples destroyed, they still remained in the hearts of these people whose lives had known as much sorrow and injustice as any on earth. Then Maha began teaching one of the central verses of the Buddha, first in Pali then in Cambodian, reciting the words over and over:

> *Hatred never ceases by hatred*
> *But by love alone is healed.*
> *This is an ancient and eternal law.*

As he chanted these verses over and over thousands began to chant with him. They chanted and wept. It was an amazing moment, for it was clear that their hearts longed for this forgiveness like a parched desert.

Maha said, that he "does not question that loving one's oppressors - Cambodians loving the Khmer Rouge - may be the most difficult attitude to achieve," then added, "But it is the law of the universe that retaliation, hatred and revenge only continue the cycle."

A Simple Lesson

MANY ZEN PUPILS WERE STUDYING meditation under the Zen Buddhist master Sengai. One of them used to arise at night, climb over the temple wall, and go to town on a pleasure jaunt.

Sengai, inspecting the dormitory quarters, found this pupil missing one night and also discovered the high stool he had used to scale the wall. Sengai removed the stool and stood there in its place.

When the wanderer returned, not knowing that Sengai was the stool, he put his feet on the master's head and jumped down into the grounds. Discovering what he had done, he was aghast.

Sengai said, "It is very chilly in the early morning. Do be careful not to catch cold yourself."

The pupil never went out at night again.

Life Without Titles

KEICHU, THE GREAT ZEN BUDDHIST teacher of the Meiji era, was the head of Tofuku, a cathedral in Kyoto. One day the governor of Kyoto called upon him for the first time.

His attendant presented the card of the governor, which read: Kitagaki, Governor of Kyoto.

"I have no business with such a fellow," said Keichu to his attendant. "Tell him to get out of here."

The attendant carried the card back with apologies.

"That was my error," said the governor, and with a pencil he scratched out the words *Governor of Kyoto*.

"Ask your teacher again."

"Oh, is that Kitagaki?" exclaimed the teacher when he saw the card. "I want to see that fellow."

It Will Pass

A YOUNG BUDDHIST STUDENT went to his meditation teacher.

"My meditation is horrible!" he said. ""I feel so distracted, and my legs ache, and I'm constantly falling asleep. This practice is worthless!"

The old Zen master listened quietly to the new monk. He nodded his head in sympathy.

"Don't worry," he said. "It will pass."

A few months later, the student came back to his teacher.

"My meditation is wonderful! I feel so aware, so peaceful, I'm alive! It's just wonderful!'

The old Zen master listened quietly to the new monk. He nodded his head.

"Don't worry," he said "It will pass."

The Champion Archer

AFTER WINNING SEVERAL ARCHERY contests, the young and rather boastful champion challenged a Zen master who was renowned for his skill as an archer. The young man demonstrated remarkable technical proficiency when he hit a distant bull's eye on his first try, and then split that arrow with his second shot.

"There," he said to the old man, "See if you can match that!"

Undisturbed, the master did not draw his bow, but rather motioned for the young archer to follow him up the mountain. Curious about the old fellow's intentions, the champion followed him high into the mountain until they reached a deep chasm spanned by a rather flimsy and shaky log. Calmly stepping out onto the middle of the unsteady and certainly perilous bridge, the old master picked a faraway tree as a target, drew his bow, and fired a clean, direct hit.

"Now it is your turn," he said as he gracefully stepped back onto the safe ground. Staring with terror into the seemingly bottomless and beckoning abyss, the young man could not force himself to even step out onto the log, let alone shoot at a target.

The master observed "You have great control over your bow, but little with the mind that lets loose the arrow."

The Poisoned Arrow

THE BUDDHA ALWAYS TOLD his disciples not to waste their time and energy in metaphysical speculation. Whenever he was asked a metaphysical question, he remained silent. Instead, he directed his disciples toward practical efforts.

Questioned one day about the problem of the infinity of the world, the Buddha said, "Whether the world is finite or infinite, limited or unlimited, the problem of your liberation remains the same."

Another time he said, 'Suppose a man is struck by a poisoned arrow and the doctor wishes to take out the arrow immediately. Suppose the man does not want the arrow removed until he knows who shot it, his age, his parents, and why he shot it. What would happen? If he were to wait until all these questions have been answered, the man might die first."

"Life is so short. It must not be spent in endless metaphysical speculation that does not bring us any closer to the truth."

The Second Arrow

ONE DAY THE BUDDHA WAS talking to a group of monks about our habit of being down on ourselves when something goes wrong, and how that only imprisons us in suffering.

Noticing that one of the young monks looked puzzled, he invited him forward and asked, "If a person is struck by an arrow, is it painful?"

The monk responded, "Well, yes it is!"

Nodding, the Buddha went on.

"And if that same person is then struck by a second arrow, would that be even more painful?"

The monk replied, "Yes, it would be."

The Buddha then explained, "In life, difficulty naturally arises - things don't go as we wish, or we have an accident, or we get sick. We can't always control that first painful arrow. However," he went on "we can add to our pain by the way we react to what's happening."

He added that we might feel victimised or angry about life being unfair, or we might blame ourselves for our poor self-care. "Our reaction is the second arrow, and it intensifies our suffering," said the Buddha. "We become identified with a suffering self."

The young monk nodded, now understanding how painful the added emotional reactivity can be.

The Buddha explained, "In life, we can't always control the first arrow. However, the second arrow is our reaction to the first. The second arrow is optional."

Separate Realities

A ZEN MASTER AND HIS one-eyed student lived together in a Buddhist temple.

One day a wondering monk came to the Zen master and said, "If you will accept me, I wish to study with you."

The old master replied, "Decide first if you belong here. Go into the garden and speak with my student. Converse with him in any way you wish. After that, come and tell me your decision."

The visiting monk nervously went out into the garden and saw the one-eyed monk meditating.

"I will show him how profound I can be," thought the visitor. "I will converse with him in sign language."

Approaching quietly, the visiting monk tapped the one-eyed monk on the shoulder and held up one finger. The one-eyed monk held up two fingers. In response, the visiting monk held up three fingers. The one-eyed monk held up his fist. When the visiting monk saw this, he dashed out of the garden to tell the old master his decision.

He came upon the old master at his chores and gasped, "I do not deserve to stay here! I am unworthy of being a fellow student with the enlightened young monk I met in the garden!"

The old master paused in his work and asked incredulously, "Are you speaking of the young one-eyed monk in the garden?"

"Yes!" exclaimed the visitor. "His knowledge is far superior to mine. I will humbly leave."

"Please tell me what happened in the garden," said the master, wide-eyed with amazement.

The visitor explained, "I approached the venerable monk and decided to converse in sign language. I held up one finger to indicate the Buddha, whereupon he held up two fingers to indicate the Buddha and his teaching, the Dharma. I persevered in the discussion, however, and held up three fingers to show the Buddha, the Dharma, and the Sangha, the community. Then he revealed the limitations of my understanding. He held up his fist to show me that they are all one. I immediately ran here to tell you I must leave."

With a large sigh, he turned and left the temple.

A moment later the young one-eyed monk stumbled into the temple. He grumbled and shouted, "Where is that scoundrel? How dare he insult me?"

"Calm your temper," said the old master. "Please tell me what happened in the garden."

The young monk explained, "I was peacefully meditating when that rude visitor interrupted my concentration. When I looked up at him, he held up one finger, indicating that I only have one eye. I held up two fingers, politely congratulating him that he has two eyes. Then he insulted me further! He held up three fingers, pointing out that there were only three eyes among. I could bear it no longer. I raised my fist to punch him on the nose and he ran away!"

Blowing In The Wind

As the Zen master approached the monastery gates at the conclusion of his morning walk, he overheard two young monks arguing about the temple flag above them.

The two monks were looking up at the flag of the monastery blowing in the wind and debating.

One of them argued, "It's the flag that is moving."

But the other insisted, "No it's the wind that is moving!"

The two young monks stopped their argument abruptly upon seeing their master. They bowed respectfully and told him about their dispute.

"Is it the flag or the wind that is moving?" they asked.

The Zen master smiled knowingly.

"It is neither," he said. "It is only your mind that is moving."

No Work, No Food

HYAKUJO, THE CHINESE ZEN MASTER, used to labour with his pupils even at the age of eighty, trimming the gardens, cleaning the grounds, and pruning the trees.

The pupils felt sorry to see the old teacher working so hard, but they knew he would not listen to their advice to stop, so they hid his tools away.

That day the master did not eat. The next day he did not eat, nor the next.

"He may be angry because we have hidden his tools," the pupils surmised.

"We had better put them back."

The day they did, the teacher worked and ate the same as before. In the evening he instructed them,

"No work, no food."

The Galloping Horse

A MONK WAS SITTING QUIETLY on the side of the road. Suddenly a man riding a horse came galloping through at full speed, almost running the monk over.

The monk was startled. He jumped to his feet and yelled at the rider, "Hey! Where are you going, in such a hurry?"

"I really don't know!" apologised the man. "Ask the horse!"

The Way Out Of Fear

ONCE THERE WAS A YOUNG student monk. Her master told her that she had to do battle with fear. She didn't want to do that. It seemed too aggressive; it was scary; it seemed unfriendly. But the master said she had to do it and gave her the instructions for the battle.

The day arrived.

The student monk stood on one side, and fear stood on the other. The student monk was feeling very small, and fear was looking big and wrathful.

The young monk roused herself and went toward fear, prostrated three times, and asked, "May I have permission to go into battle with you?"

Fear said, "Thank you for showing me so much respect that you ask permission."

Then the young monk asked, "How can I defeat you?"

Fear replied, "My weapons are that I talk fast, and I get very close to your face. Then you get completely unnerved, and you do whatever I say. If you don't do what I tell you, I have no power. You can listen to me, and you can have respect for me. You can even be convinced by me. But if you don't do what I say, I have no power."

That day, the student monk learned how to defeat fear.

Say Yes

A MAN WENT TO A BUDDHIST monastery for a silent retreat. After he finished, he felt better, calmer and stronger, but something was missing.

The master said he could talk to one of the monks before he left.

The man thought for a while, then asked, "How do you find peace?"

The monk said, "I say yes, to everything that happens, I just say yes."

The man returned home, enlightened.

The Bowl

A MONK TOLD THE MASTER, "I have just entered the monastery. Please teach me."

The master asked, "Have you eaten your rice porridge?"

The monk replied, "I have eaten."

The master said, "Then you had better wash your bowl."

At that moment the monk was enlightened.

Lighting The Candles

ONE RAINY DAY THE KING summoned the local monk master to his palace. He was pondering life and wanted advice from the wise master.

"Am I the same person I was when I was a child?" he asked.

"That is a very wise question. What does your gut tell you?" replied the monk.

"Well," said the king after a short pause, "the body was obviously different back then, and so was the mind. But it seems like there was something that remained the same all along."

"That is close to the truth," the monk nodded. "But in fact, you are neither the same nor different from that child long ago."

"How is it possible to be neither the same nor different?" asked the king.

"Allow me to illustrate it for you," offered the monk.

"Imagine a long line of white candles. The first candle in the line is used to light up the second candle, the second candle is used to light up the third candle, and the third is used to light the fourth, and so on until all candles are lit.

Now what do you think, great king? Is the fire that lights up the first candle the same or different from the fire that lights up the second candle? Is it the same or different from the fire that lights up the last candle?"

The Four Candles

FOUR MONKS DECIDED TO meditate silently without speaking for two weeks. They lit a candle as a symbol of their practice and began. By nightfall on the first day, the candle flickered and then went out.

The first monk said, "Oh, no! The candle is out!"

The second monk said, "We're not supposed to talk!"

The third monk said, "Why must you two break the silence?"

The fourth monk laughed and said, "Ha! I'm the only one who didn't speak."

The Crystal Cup

A ZEN MASTER WAS GIVEN A beautifully crafted crystal cup. It was a gift from a former student.

He was very grateful. Every day, he enjoyed drinking out of his glass. He would show it to visitors and tell them about the kindness of his student.

But every morning, he held the cup in his hand for a few seconds and reminded himself, "This glass is already broken."

One day, a clumsy visitor toppled the glass from its shelf. The cup fell down and when it hit the floor, it smashed into thousands of tiny pieces.

The other visitors gasped in shock, but the Zen master remained calm. Looking at the mess in front of his feet, he happily picked up a broom and started sweeping.

The Zen master later shared with his students, "The man who remembers to be grateful for his possessions is ahead of most. But the man who knows they won't last forever, is ahead of him still."

The Empty Boat

ONE DAY A STUDENT MONK decided to meditate alone, away from his monastery. He took his boat out to the middle of the lake, moored it, closed his eyes and began his meditation. After a few hours of undisturbed silence, he suddenly felt the bump of another boat colliding with his own.

With his eyes still closed, he sensed his anger rising, and by the time he opened his eyes, he was ready to scream at the boatman who dared disturb his meditation. But when he opened his eyes, he saw it was an empty boat that had probably got untethered and floated out to the middle of the lake.

At that moment, the monk had an insight and understood that the anger was within him; it merely needed the bump of an external object to provoke it out of him. From then on, whenever he came across someone who irritated him or provoked him to anger, he reminded himself.

"The other person is merely an empty boat. The anger is within me…"

The Four Wives

ONCE THERE WAS A WEALTHY MAN who had four wives. The man was old, had become ill and was about to die. At the end of his life, he felt very lonely and so asked the first wife to accompany him to the other world.

'My dear wife,' he said, 'I loved you day and night, I took care of you throughout my whole life. Now I am about to die, will you please go with me wherever I go after my death?'

He expected her to answer yes.

But she answered, 'My dear husband, I know you always loved me. And you are going to die. Now it is time to separate from you. Goodbye, my dear.'

He called his second wife to his sickbed and begged her to follow him in death.

He said, 'My dear second wife, you know how I loved you. Sometimes I was afraid you might leave me, but I held on to you strongly. My dear, please come with me.'

The second wife expressed herself rather coldly. 'Dear husband, your first wife refused to accompany you after your death. How can I follow you? You loved me only for your own selfish sake.'

Lying on his deathbed, he called his third wife, and asked her to follow him.

The third wife replied, with tears in her eyes, 'My dear, I pity you and I feel sad for myself. Therefore I shall accompany you to the graveyard. This is my last duty to you.' The third wife thus also refused to follow him to death.

Three wives had refused to follow him after his death. Now he called for his fourth wife, for whom he didn't care very much. He had never paid much attention to her and had treated her like a slave. But now he was desperate.

The fourth wife gladly accepted her husband's request.

'My dear husband,' she said, 'I will go with you. Whatever happens, I am determined to be with you forever. We will never be separated.'

"Now, who are these four wives?" asked the Buddha, then explained,

"The first 'wife' is the body. The man loved it and took care of it his whole life. But the reality is it can't follow us into the next world. It must be given back to the earth from which it came.

The second wife represents all material things such as property, fame, position, and money. The man pursued it and held onto it tightly all his life, but it couldn't escort him to death.

The third wife is our family and society. They could stand by the man throughout his life, but upon death, they could only accompany him to the graveyard.

The message here is that we can't take our body, wealth, or family with us in the end.

And the fourth wife is the man's karma. For only the consequences of his good and harmful deeds will follow him forever."

That Damn Stick

YAMAOKA TESSHU, A YOUNG STUDENT of Zen Buddhism, visited one master after another accumulating knowledge from them all. Soon enough, he called upon Zen master Dokuon of Shokoku.

Desiring to show off his wisdom, Tesshu said, "The mind, Buddha, and all sentient beings do not exist. The true nature of phenomena is emptiness. There is no realization, no delusion, no master, no Buddha. There is no giving and nothing to be received."

Dokuon, who was sitting and smoking quietly, said nothing. Suddenly he whacked Yamaoka on the head with his bamboo stick. This made the young monk quite angry.

"Why did you hit me with that damn stick!?"

"If nothing exists," said Dokuon, "What is this damn stick you speak of?"

83 Problems

THERE'S AN OLD STORY ABOUT A man who came to see
the Buddha because he had heard that the Buddha
was a great teacher. Like all of us, he had some
problems in his life, and he thought the Buddha
might be able to help him straighten those out.

He told the Buddha that he was a farmer.

"I like farming," he said, "but sometimes it
doesn't rain enough, and my crops fail. Last year
we nearly starved. And sometimes it rains too
much, so my yields aren't what I'd like then to be."

The Buddha patiently listened to the man.

"I'm married too," said the man. "She's a
good wife… I love her in fact. But sometimes she
nags me too much. And sometimes I get tired of
her."

The Buddha listened quietly.

"I have kids," said the man. "Good kids,
too… but sometimes they don't show me enough
respect. And sometimes…"

The man went on like this, laying out his
difficulties and worries. Finally he wound down

and waited for the Buddha to say the words that would put everything right for him.

Instead the Buddha said, "I can't help you."

"What do you mean?" said the astonished man.

"Everybody's got problems," said the Buddha. "In fact, we've all got 83 problems. 83 problems and there's nothing you can do about it. If you work really hard on one of them, maybe you can fix it - but if you do, another one will pop right into its place. For example, you're going to lose your loved ones eventually. And you're going to die someday. Now there's a problem, and there's nothing you or I, or anyone else, can do about it."

The man became furious. "I thought you were a great teacher," he shouted. "I thought you could help me! What good are your teachings then?"

The Buddha said, "Well, maybe they will help you with the 84th problem."

"The 84th problem?" said the man. "What's the 84th problem?"

"You want to not have any problems," said Buddha.

Thank You For Everything

HUNDREDS OF YEARS AGO in Japan, a Zen master named Sono was known far and wide for her wisdom. Many came to her to find healing for their bodies, their minds, and their hearts. But no matter what their pain or affliction, Sono offered one simple remedy.

"Every day repeat this mantra: Thank you for everything, I have no complaints whatsoever."

As the story goes, those who took her wise advice to heart found happiness and healing.

What We Seek Is What We Find

TWO MEN VISITED A ZEN MASTER.

The first man said, "I'm thinking of moving to this town. What's it like?"

The Zen master asked, "What was your old town like?"

The first man responded, "It was dreadful, everyone was hateful. I hated it, hence I wish to move."

The Zen master said, "This town is very similar. I don't think you should move here."

The first man left and the second man entered.

The second man said, "I'm thinking of moving to this town. What's it like?"

The Zen master asked, "What was your old town like?"

The second man responded, "It was wonderful. Everyone was friendly, I was very happy. I'm just interested in a change now."

The Zen master said, "This town is very similar. I think you will like it here."

True Happiness And Prosperity

A RICH MAN ASKED A ZEN MASTER to write something down that could encourage the prosperity of his family for years to come. It would be something that the family could cherish for generations.

On a large piece of paper, the master wrote, "Father dies, son dies, grandson dies."

The rich man became angry when he saw the master's work. "I asked you to write something down that could bring happiness and prosperity to my family. Why do you give me something depressing like this?"

"If your son should die before you," the master answered, "this would bring unbearable grief to your family. If your grandson should die before your son, this also would bring great sorrow. If your family, generation after generation, disappears in the order I have described, it will be the natural course of life. This is true happiness and prosperity."

Buddha And
The Businessman

A BUSINESSMAN ONCE CAME into Buddha's assembly, and spat at Buddha. He was furious that his children who could have spent their time earning money, meditated with Buddha instead.

Buddha merely smiled at him. There was no word, no reaction. The man walked away in a huff, shocked. He could not sleep all night. For the first time in his life, he met someone who smiled when he was spat at. His whole world had turned upside down.

The next day he went back to Buddha, fell at his feet and said, "Please forgive me! I didn't know what I did."

But Buddha said,, "No! I cannot excuse you!"

Everyone in his assembly was taken aback!

Buddha said, "Why should I forgive you when you have done nothing wrong?"

The businessman reminded him of what he did on the previous day.

Buddha simply replied, "Oh that person is not here now. If I ever meet the person you spat on, I'll tell him to excuse you. To this person here, you've not done any wrong."

The World Mirrors The Heart

A YOUNG STUDENT MONK PRIDED himself on his wit and liked to debate his Buddhist master. One day, over tea, he challenged the master.

"Master, people think you are an enlightened monk, but to me you just look like a big, stinking pile of worthless dung sitting on your pillow all day long."

The student monk leaned backward and crossed his arms slyly.

The master placed his hands in prayer position, "My dear, but to me you look like a Buddha."

The student monk grinned and bid the master farewell.

When the student got home, he was wearing a triumphant smile. His sister asked him what happened.

"Today I outsmarted the Master," he replied, then recounted the events to her.

"Oh no, brother! I'm sorry to tell you this, but you lost badly," she said.

"What do you mean?"

"Don't you realize that the world mirrors the heart? The Master sees you as a Buddha because he is a Buddha. You see him as a pile of dung. What does that make you?"

The student turned the colour of beetroot. Then, all of a sudden, he became enlightened.

Judging Others

ONCE THERE WAS A ZEN MASTER who used to go door to door asking for food. He always went dressed in rags with an empty bowl in his hands.

One day he went to the door of a rich man. The rich man, seeing his ragged clothes, returned his empty bowl.

The next day the same master went back to the rich man's house but this time he was wearing his formal monk's robe. This time the rich man invited him in and served up a sumptuous meal.

The master removed his robe and folded it. He placed it on front of the feast served by the rich man and got up.

The rich man was confused by this and questioned. "What are you doing?"

The master replied, "This meal is for the robe, not for me," and left.

Nature's Perfection

A MONK WAS IN CHARGE OF THE garden within a famous Zen temple. He had been given the job because he loved the flowers, shrubs, and trees. Next to the temple there was another, smaller temple where there lived a very old Zen master. One day, when the priest was expecting some special guests, he took extra care in tending to the garden. He pulled the weeds, trimmed the shrubs, combed the moss, and spent a long time meticulously raking up and carefully arranging all the dry autumn leaves.

As he worked, the old master watched him with interest from across the wall that separated the temples. When he had finished, the monk stood back to admire his work.

"Isn't it beautiful," he called out to the old master.

"Yes," replied the old man, "but there is something missing. Help me over this wall and I'll put it right for you."

After hesitating, the priest lifted the old fellow over and set him down.

Slowly, the master walked to the tree near the centre of the garden, grabbed it by the trunk, and shook it. Leaves showered down all over the garden.

"There," said the old man, "you can put me back now."

Chasing Two Rabbits

A YOUNG ZEN STUDENT APPROACHED his master with a question.

"I'd like to accelerate my knowledge of Zen. In addition to learning from you, I'd like to study with another teacher. What do you think of this idea?"

"He who chases two rabbits," answered the master, "catches none."

Leave No Trace

ONE OF THE PRACTICES IN SOME Buddhist monasteries is to wash, towel-dry, and put used cups and dishes back where they belong as part of the 'leave no trace' training.

A young student monk on seeing that other residents occasionally left their dishes in the sink, did what he thought was the right thing to do and put them away.

The master caught him one day and said, "How are you helping them with their practice if you do that for them? Leave the dishes for them to see when they return."

The master went on to explain. "Even an act of kindness can have a negative impact. Sometimes we cause more damage by trying to help because we're not looking at the big picture of what 'helping' truly means."

The Chess Game

A PRINCE WENT TO A ZEN MASTER and told him that he wanted to be enlightened - right away!

Instead of sending him away, the master said it could be arranged. After finding out from the prince that he played chess very well, the master set up a game between the visitor and one of his monks who had just a passing knowledge of chess. The condition was: whoever loses will be beheaded.

Predictably, the prince started dominating the game. Soon, however, his conscience started to prick him.

"I had come to this monastery for a selfish purpose, but now I may become the cause of this poor monk's death."

So, feeling compassionate, he deliberately started playing badly. But playing well was second nature to him, playing badly needed his entire attention. Neither did he want to play too bad a game to make his real move obvious. His nerves stretched, soon he started sweating profusely. After some time, the master stopped the game.

"The first lesson is over," he told the prince. "You learnt two things today: compassion and concentration. Now go and hug your chess opponent who made it all possible."

All We Have Is Now

A ZEN WARRIOR WAS CAPTURED by his enemies and thrown into prison.

That night he was unable to sleep because he feared that the next day he would be interrogated, tortured, and executed.

Then the words of his Zen master came to him.

"Tomorrow is not real. It is an illusion. The only reality is now."

Heeding these words, the warrior became peaceful and fell asleep.

Transient

A FAMOUS ZEN MASTER CAME to the front door of the King's palace.

None of the guards tried to stop him as he entered and made his way to where the King himself was sitting on his throne.

"What do you want?" asked the King, recognizing the master.

"I would like a place to sleep in this inn," replied the master.

"But this is not an inn," said the King, "It is my palace."

"May I ask who owned this palace before you?"

"My father. He is dead."

"And who owned it before him?"

"My grandfather. He too is dead."

"And this place where people live for a short time and then move on - did I hear you say that it is NOT an inn?"

The Tea Ceremony

A MASTER OF THE TEA CEREMONY in old Japan once accidentally insulted a soldier. He quickly apologized, but the rather impetuous soldier demanded that the matter be settled in a sword duel.

The tea master, who had no experience with swords, asked the advice of a fellow Zen master who did possess such skill.

As he was served by his friend, the Zen swordsman could not help but notice how the tea master performed his art with perfect concentration and tranquillity.

"Tomorrow," the Zen swordsman said, "when you duel the soldier, hold your weapon above your head, as if ready to strike, and face him with the same concentration and tranquillity with which you perform the tea ceremony."

The next day, at the appointed time and place for the duel, the tea master followed this advice. The soldier, readying himself to strike, stared for a long time into the fully attentive but calm face of the tea master.

Finally, the soldier lowered his sword, apologized for his arrogance, and left without a blow being struck.

Egotism

THE PRIME MINISTER OF THE Tang Dynasty was a national hero for his success as both a statesman and military leader. But despite his fame, power, and wealth, he considered himself a humble and devout Buddhist.

Often he visited a Zen master to study under him, and they seemed to get along very well. The fact that he was prime minister apparently had no effect on their relationship, which seemed to be simply one of a revered master and respectful student.

One day, during his usual visit, the Prime Minister asked the master, "Your Reverence, what is egotism according to Buddhism?"

The master's face turned red, and in a very condescending and insulting tone of voice, he shot back, "What kind of stupid question is that!?"

This unexpected response so shocked the Prime Minister that he became sullen and angry. The Zen master then smiled and said, "THIS, Your Excellency, is egotism."

Prison

FOR SEVERAL WEEKS A BUDDHIST Monk had been teaching meditation in a maximum-security prison. The small group of prisoners had come to know and respect the monk well. At the end of one session, they began to ask him about his routine in a Buddhist monastery.

"We have to get up a 4.00 a.m. every morning," he began. "Sometimes it is very cold because our small rooms don't have heaters. We eat only one meal a day, all mixed together in the one bowl. In the afternoon and at night-time we can eat nothing at all. There is no sex or alcohol, of course. Nor do we have television, radio or music. We never watch movies, nor can we play sport. We talk little, work hard and spend our free time sitting cross-legged watching our breath. And we sleep on the floor."

The inmates were stunned at the Spartan austerity of the monastic life. It made their high-security prison appear like a five-star hotel in comparison.

In fact, one of the prisoners was so moved with sympathy for the plight of their monk friend that he forgot where he was and said, "That's terrible living in your monastery. Why don't you come in here and stay with us?"

Everyone in the room cracked up with laughter.

The Buddhist monk saw this as an opportunity to share wisdom around this subject.

"It is true that a monastery is far more ascetic than the severest of prisons for society's felons, yet many come to stay of their free will, and are happy there. Whereas many want to escape from the well-appointed prison, and are unhappy there. Why? It is because, in a monastery, the inmates want to be there; in a prison, the inmates **don't** want to be there. That is the difference. Any place you don't want to be, no matter how comfortable, is a prison for you.

This is the real meaning of the word 'prison' - any situation where you don't want to be. If you are in a job where you don't want to be, then you are in a prison. If you are in a relationship where you don't want to be, you are also in a prison. If you are in a sick and painful body where you don't want to be, then that too is a prison for you. A prison is any situation where you don't want to be."

"Freedom is being content to be where you are. Prison is wanting to be somewhere else."

A Happy Accident

THERE IS A LOVELY STORY of a Zen Master being interviewed and asked "What is Enlightenment?.

His reply is "It's a happy accident".

On his return to the monastery, his monks start to question him about his answer.

"If it's a happy accident, then why do we have to meditate for 8 hours, fast for days at a time, and do all these other exercises?

The Zen Master laughs and replies "To increase the possibility of the accident".

OTHER BOOKS BY BARRY

Life Changing Quotes, 2013

How You Can Write a Great First Book, 2018

Inspirational and Motivational Short Stories, 2019

A Better Way to Live, 2022

Ingram Content Group UK Ltd.
Milton Keynes UK
UKHW020620040523
421215UK00010B/254

9 781739 713911